T0004704

How Aircraft Carriers Work

Candice Ransom

Lerner Publications • Minneapolis

Lerner Publications Company
An imprint of Lerner Publishing Group, Inc.
241 First Avenue North
Minneapolis, MN 55401 USA

For reading levels and more information, look up this title at www.lernerbooks.com.

Library of Congress Cataloging-in-Publication Data

Names: Ransom, Candice F., 1952- author.
Title: How aircraft carriers work / Candice Ransom.
Description: Minneapolis : Lerner Publications, [2020] | Series: Lightning bolt books. Military
    machines | Audience: Age 6-9. | Audience: Grades K-3.
Includes bibliographical references and index.
Identifiers: LCCN 2018046166 (print) | LCCN 2018047618 (ebook) | ISBN 9781541556577 (eb
    pdf) | ISBN 9781541555679 (lb : alk. paper)
Subjects: LCSH: Aircraft carriers—Juvenile literature.
Classification: LCC V874 (ebook) | LCC V874 .R36 2020 (print) | DDC 359.9/4835—dc23

LC record available at https://lccn.loc.gov/2018046166

Manufactured in the United States of America
1-46022-43345-2/8/2019

Table of Contents

Giants of the Sea

A large ship floats in the ocean. It is an aircraft carrier. It was built as a base for jets. A jet glides down the flight deck and prepares for takeoff.

The jet has only 300 feet (91 m) of space to get into the air. A machine called a catapult helps the jet go faster. The catapult pulls the jet down the runway.

The catapult launches the jet at a speed of 170 miles (274 km) per hour.

Another jet is landing on the ship. The jet's tail has a hook. Four strong wires stretch across the ship's deck.

The pilot of the jet aims for a wire. The tailhook catches it. Then the jet lands safely on the rocking ship.

Aircraft Carrier History

In 1909, Orville and Wilbur Wright built the first plane for the military. Planes stayed at bases on the ground. They could not fly long distances.

In 1910, Eugene Ely flew an airplane off the deck of a ship. The military started building special ships where planes could take off and land.

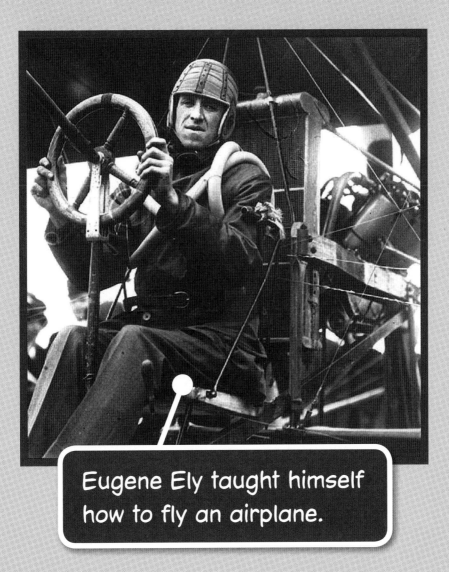

Eugene Ely taught himself how to fly an airplane.

By the 1950s, aircraft carriers could hold fast, heavy jets. Straight decks were angled so jets could take off or land at the same time.

Aircraft Carrier Parts

Aircraft carriers are about 244 feet tall (74 m). The flight deck area is 4.5 acres (1.8 ha). That's the size of three and a half football fields!

The captain controls the ship from a place called the island. The island stands on the top deck.

68

Each level of an aircraft carrier's island has command centers for officers.

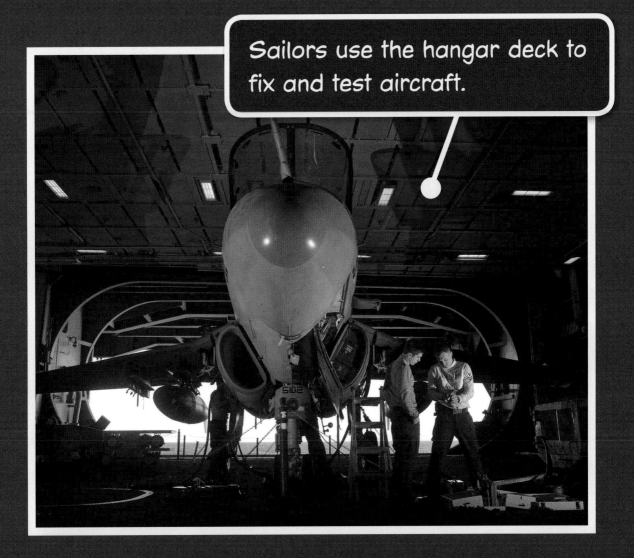

Sailors use the hangar deck to fix and test aircraft.

The hangar deck is below the flight deck. Aircraft are stored there. Giant elevators move jets from one deck to another.

The engines are in the bottom of the ship in the hull. Two nuclear reactors power the ship.

Nuclear power allows aircraft carriers to complete missions without refueling.

Anchors keep the ship from moving. They weigh 60,000 pounds (27,215 kg).

An anchor is raised and lowered very slowly by a machine called a windlass.

Aircraft Carriers in Action

Five thousand to six thousand people work on an aircraft carrier. They live on the ship for weeks.

The ship has a hospital, library, fire station, barbershop, and dining halls.

Workers on the flight deck wear shirts that are different colors. People in white shirts help land planes. Those in green shirts handle cargo.

The flight deck crew work as a team to make sure takeoffs and landings go smoothly.

Navy aircraft carriers are considered American territory. That means they are a safe base for US fighter jets. They also help other branches of the military during war.

The newest aircraft carrier is the USS *Gerald Ford*. Its nuclear reactors can keep the ship running for twenty years. What do you think aircraft carriers will look like in the future?

Aircraft Carrier Diagram

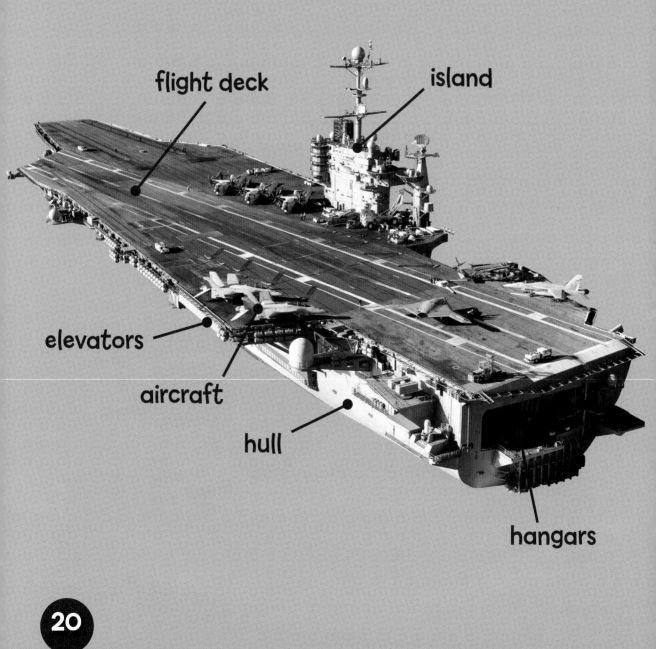

flight deck

island

elevators

aircraft

hull

hangars

Aircraft Carrier Facts

- Modern aircraft carriers are made of about a billion different parts and pieces!

- Helicopters from some aircraft carriers used to pick up astronauts that landed in the ocean when their missions were completed.

- The carrier USS *George H. W. Bush* has ninety-three cooks aboard. They prepare eighteen thousand meals a day—breakfast, lunch, dinner, and "mid rats," or midnight rations.

Glossary

anchor: a heavy iron part that keeps a ship from moving

catapult: a machine for launching planes from the deck of a ship

deck: the floor of a ship that goes from side to side

hangar: a part of a ship used to store aircraft

hull: the part of the ship that is below the water

island: the command center on aircraft carriers

nuclear: a powerful type of energy

Further Reading

Boothroyd, Jennifer. *Inside the US Navy*. Minneapolis: Lerner Publications, 2018.

Murray, Julie. *United States Navy*. Minneapolis: Abdo, 2015.

Peppas, Lynn. *Aircraft Carriers: Runways at Sea*. New York: Crabtree, 2012.

United States Navy Facts for Kids
https://kids.kiddle.co/United_States_Navy

World War II Aircraft Carriers
http://www.historyforkids.net/aircraft-carriers
-world%20war-2.html

Index

Photo Acknowledgments

Image credits: Shayne Johnson/U.S. Navy, p. 2; Angelina Grimsley/U.S. Navy, p. 4; Chad M. Trudeau/U.S. Navy, p. 5; Kurtis A. Hatcher/U.S. Navy, p. 6; Stocktrek Images/Getty Images, p. 7; US Army Corps of Engineers, p. 8; Courtesy of San Diego Air and Space Museum, p. 9; NH UA 452 12 courtesy of the Naval History & Heritage Command, p. 10; Nathan Lockwood/U.S. Navy, p. 11; Kelly M. Agee/U.S. Navy, p. 12; James R. Evans/U.S. Navy, p. 13; Nichelle N. Bishop/U.S. Navy, p. 14; Anderson W. Branch/U.S. Navy, p. 15; Trey Hutcheson/U.S. Navy, p. 16; Sean M. Castellano/U.S. Navy, p. 17; James Turner/U.S. Navy, p. 18; Julia A. Casper/U.S. Navy, p. 19; Kristina Young/U.S. Navy, p. 20; Zachary A. Anderson/U.S. Navy, p. 22.

Front cover: Stocktrek Images/Getty Images.

Main body text set in Billy Infant regular 28/36. Typeface provided by SparkType.

Aircraft carriers are big and strong military watercraft. But did you know that they use catapults to launch jets? Or that they can be fueled by nuclear power? Find out more in this look at these impressive machines!

LIGHTNING BOLT BOOKS™

Learn about different military vehicles in the Military Machines series—part of the Lightning Bolt Books® collection. With high-energy designs, appealing photos, and lively text, Lightning Bolt Books® bring nonfiction topics to life!

Military Machines
How Aircraft Carriers Work
How Drones Work
How Fighter Jets Work
How Military Helicopters Work
How Submarines Work
How Tanks Work

ISBN 978-1-5415-7454-0

Lerner™
www.lernerbooks.com
GRL: 0

9 781541 574540